CALIFORNIA
MISSIONS

Discovering Mission San José

BY MADELINE STEVENS

Cavendish
Square

New York

Published in 2015 by Cavendish Square Publishing, LLC
243 5th Avenue, Suite 136, New York, NY 10016

Copyright © 2015 by Cavendish Square Publishing, LLC

First Edition

CPSIA Compliance Information: Batch #WS14CSQ

All websites were available and accurate when this book was sent to press.

Library of Congress Cataloging-in-Publication Data

Stevens, Madeline.
Discovering Mission San José / Madeline Stevens.
pages cm. — (California missions)
Includes index.
ISBN 978-1-62713-064-6 (hardcover) ISBN 978-1-62713-066-0 (ebook)
1. Mission San Jose (Alameda County, Calif.)—History—Juvenile literature. 2. Ohlone Indians—Missions—California—Alameda County—History—Juvenile literature. 3. California—History—To 1846—Juvenile literature. I. Title.

F869.M66S74 2014
979.4'65—dc23

2014005333

Editorial Director: Dean Miller
Editor: Kristen Susienka
Copy Editor: Cynthia Roby
Art Director: Jeffrey Talbot
Designer: Douglas Brooks
Photo Researcher: J8 Media
Production Manager: Jennifer Ryder-Talbot
Production Editor: David McNamara

Printed in the United States of America

CALIFORNIA
MISSIONS

Contents

Mission San José was part of a mission system whose influence helped shape California's history.

1
The Spanish in America

ONE OF THE MOST SUCCESSFUL MISSIONS

Nestled between rolling hills just outside the city of San José is a small white building with a brown roof. Numerous steps made of red brick lead to the building's entrance: a simple door with two small windows above. This is Mission San José, the fourteenth of twenty-one Spanish **missions** to be built along the California coast during the eighteenth and nineteenth centuries. The mission was founded in 1797 by Fray Fermín Francisco Lausén, a Spanish friar (or *fray* in Spanish). Known to have been one of the most successful missions on the northern coast, it flourished until 1832. The story of how it came to be is interesting and full of prosperity, struggle, and hardship.

AGE OF EXPLORERS

In 1492, Christopher Columbus, an Italian explorer sailing for Spain, was trying to find a quick route from Europe to Asia. Instead, he encountered what would come to be referred to as the Caribbean and the New World (North America, South America, and Central America), which he **claimed** for Spain. His return to Spain led many others to follow in his footsteps. Men such as Hernán Cortés, Juan Rodríguez Cabrillo, and Sebastián Vizcaíno each made significant discoveries in the New World over the next few decades. These discoveries expanded the Spanish empire across the seas.

In 1519, Hernán Cortés and his men sailed to South America and encountered the powerful and wealthy Aztec empire, which they conquered in 1521 and won land for the crown of Spain. Later, in 1542, explorer Juan Rodríguez Cabrillo set out to explore the western coast of California, in the hope of finding a way to connect the Pacific and Atlantic Oceans. He never found the water route, however, and sadly died on this remarkable journey. Still, Cabrillo is known as one of the first Spanish explorers of California, and he claimed much of what is now the state of California for Spain. What was "California" at that time consisted of what is known today as the state of California and the Baja Peninsula of Mexico. It was divided into two parts: *Alta*, or upper, California and *Baja*, or lower, California.

Another Spanish explorer, Sebastián Vizcaíno, made the same journey as Cabrillo in 1602. It was then that he encountered Native people but no treasures such as those found by Cortés in 1519. The Spanish government then decided not to continue exploration of the area. It would be 160 years until Spanish explorers would again travel to **Alta California**—this time to form missions that would take over the land and **convert** the Native people to Christianity and the Spanish way of life.

2
The Ohlone

ENCOUNTERING THE INDIGENOUS PEOPLE

When the Spanish explorers arrived in the western part of the New World, they encountered many different tribes, or groups, of Native people. The Ohlone was the most dominant and diverse group, and one that had lived near the area where Mission San José was established.

The Ohlone tribe lived in separate villages from the other groups. They spoke different languages and dialects but had no written language. Most of their villages were located around the San Francisco Bay area, and prior to the arrival of the Spanish, they lived relatively peacefully. They were a generous and curious group of people, who enjoyed making tools by using what resources they had around them. They made everything from bows and arrows to baskets and boats, and even musical instruments.

The Ohlone weaved unique baskets that could carry items such as food and water.

The Ohlone people lived in villages that were run by leaders called chiefs and healers called shamans.

HUNTERS AND GATHERERS

The Ohlone were hunters and gatherers, depending on the animals and plants that lived around them for food. The men were skilled hunters, and they took pride in their handmade bows and arrows. All weapons and tools were made from wood, rocks, or animal bones. The men hunted deer, antelope, ducks, and geese, while the women gathered berries, roots, and seafood from the Pacific Ocean.

Out of all the natural resources the Ohlone used, they depended mostly on acorns. They used all the different acorns growing in the area, as they were easy to collect, store, and eat when prepared correctly. Often the women, who did most of the cooking, made acorn flour to bake bread and create porridge.

A WAY OF LIFE

The Ohlone lived in villages numbering from fifty to several hundred members. Every village had an assembly house and a sweathouse. Constructed from **tule**, or tightly woven reeds, the assembly house was used for large gatherings and could hold the entire village population. Individual homes were also made of tule. When a home was infested with bugs or became dirty over time, its occupants burned it down and built another in its place. The sweathouse was a small hut where the Native people cleansed their bodies through sweating. They went through this ritual for a variety of reasons, such as curing an illness, healing a skin disease, or preparing for a hunt.

The Ohlone made their own tools from resources around them, such as this mortar and pestle.

Every village was led by a chief, one of the wealthiest members of the tribe. He or she shared the wealth with everyone who needed it. It was the chief's responsibility to make sure that visitors were given food and a place to stay.

CLOTHING

What the Ohlone wore depended on the season. In the warmer months, men wore little to no clothing, while women wore skirts made from grasses and reeds. When the autumn and winter seasons arrived, the Ohlone wore animal furs for warmth.

RELIGIOUS BELIEFS AND PRACTICES

The Ohlone believed there should be a balance between humans and nature, and that certain animals, particularly large birds such as eagles, were sacred and should not be harmed or eaten. The main religious leader was called a **shaman**. The shaman could be male or female and took care of all religious matters. The tribe believed that the shaman was able to control the weather and heal sick people.

FAMILY LIFE

Ohlone tribes looked after their members with care. Children were not just raised by their mothers and fathers but by their extended families as well. The older tribespeople were treated with great respect and the younger members listened to them carefully. Days in the village were usually spent gathering, hunting, and preparing food. Children and adults had plenty of time to play.

XII

In the early 1800s, Russian traders visited California. Louis Choris, an artist with them, drew these sketches of the Native people who lived there.

In their villages, the Ohlone could live as they pleased, without a strict schedule. They did what they needed to survive, and they spent their free time enjoying life. Their curious and hard-working natures likely made it easy for Spanish **missionaries** to enter their lives in the late 1700s.

When the Spanish arrived, little did the Ohlone know their lifestyles and cultures would change forever.

3
The
Mission System

THE SPANISH EXTEND THEIR INFLUENCE

By the year 1797, when Mission San José was founded, thirteen other missions had already been started in Alta California. Each mission was guided by Spanish missionaries, or **friars**. Over time, the missions would gradually become thriving communities.

WHY THE MISSIONS WERE STARTED

When the Spanish resumed journeying to the New World in the mid to late 1700s, they were not searching for gold or other special objects. They wanted to claim more land for the ever-growing Spanish empire, and to convert the Native people into Christians and eventually into subjects of Spain. They did not understand the Native peoples' way of life and believed that the Native people could live well only if they lived like Spaniards. Missions, or religious communities, were established in Baja California and later Alta California. They would house the Native people and the friars would teach them about the Christian god, how to farm, take care of livestock, and speak Spanish. When Native people converted, they were baptized, or immersed in water as a symbol of their belief in the Christian god. They were then considered **neophytes**, or new converts.

THE MISSIONS IN ALTA CALIFORNIA

The missions started because the Spanish government wanted to explore and secure more land in Alta California before other countries, such as Russia and Britain, could move into the area. The idea was to establish a chain of missions along the West Coast, all connected by a road, *El Camino Real*. Some armies accompanied the missionaries to help ward off anyone who might attack them, as well as to set up their own military fortresses,

The Historic Missions, Presidios & Pueblos of California

Twenty-one missions and four presidios were built along the coast of California, all connected by a road called El Camino Real (illustrated by the yellow line).

called *presidios*. Non-missionaries, or settlers, also traveled with these groups to start *pueblos*, or towns.

ECONOMY OF THE MISSIONS

Each mission developed an economy so that people who were a part of the mission system were **self-sufficient**. As more people came to live and work at a mission, its economy became stronger, enabling its growth. The Spanish thought that after ten years the missions could be **secularized**, or turned from religious institutions into civic ones. The intention was to give the mission lands over to the neophytes, who by that time were tax-paying Spanish citizens and would care for them. But this did not happen as the missionaries planned. The Spanish government was no longer in control after 1821—when Mexico gained its independence—and the lands of Alta California fell under Mexican rule.

Mission San José was the fourteenth mission founded in Alta California.

4
The Founding of Mission San José

MOVING MISSIONS CLOSER TO THE NATIVES

By the time Mission San José started in 1797, the Alta California missions were already well established. They had begun in 1769, with Mission San Diego de Alcalá, and had grown to a total of thirteen before Mission San José came along. The founder of Mission San José was Fray Fermín Francisco Lasuén. He had taken over heading all of the missions in 1784 after the first mission's leader, Fray Junípero Serra—the man who developed the mission chain—died. In 1795, Fray Lasuén stated that new missions should be located closer to the Native tribes of the area. The village where Mission San José would be constructed was Orisom, a place where many Ohlone tribes lived. Orisom had a few rocky areas, good land for growing crops, and was close to a source of water—the Alameda Creek. All this made the village a desirable location for the friars to go to and start preaching.

FRAY ISIDRO BARCENILLA AND AGUSTÍN MERINO

Fray Lasuén was officially the founder of Mission San José—that is, it was created while he was mission president. The first friars leading the mission were Fray Isidro Barcenilla and Agustín Merino. Both were new graduates of the College of San Fernando de Mexico, located in New Spain (present-day Mexico). Being energetic about reaching out to the Native people, they worked together to convert the Ohlone.

MISSION SAN JOSÉ

Mission San José was founded on June 11, 1797. This was thirteen years after the death of Fray Serra, but his memory lived on as the missions continued to be built along Alta California's coast. Fray Fermín Lasuén named the mission after Saint Joseph, the husband of Jesus's mother, Mary. A brief religious service, called a Mass, and a dedication were held to welcome the new community.

Within forty-eight hours of the founding service, shelters were quickly constructed. Soldiers from San Francisco and neophytes from Mission Santa Clara de Asís did most of the work. Soon after, Mission Santa Clara de Asís and Mission San Francisco de Asís sent supplies and livestock to help Mission San José get started. The workers built houses for the priests and neophytes, and a temporary chapel. The official chapel would not be dedicated until 1809.

THE MISSION AND THE OHLONE

When the Spanish arrived, the Ohlone people living near the area were curious but did not welcome the idea of the mission or what the friars tried to teach them. The Ohlone had firm religious beliefs, and valued family and nature. They believed in

Native Americans lived in California for thousands of years before European settlers arrived.

a Creator and that all living things—animals, plants, and Earth itself—held spirits. The idea of Christianity, and that land could be owned, was a difficult concept for the Ohlone to embrace. The missionaries persisted with delivering their message although it was difficult because each Ohlone tribe spoke a different language. The friars could not understand the Ohlone, who in turn could not understand the friars. In its first year, only thirty-three Ohlone joined Mission San José. This number was low but about average for the early days of any mission. More started joining when the friars offered them new clothes, blankets, and food. Before long, some were being baptized and started living in the mission buildings, but they were not always happy.

The neophytes were told that they must live at the mission, only occasionally being allowed to visit their old villages. As time went on, the missionaries made it nearly impossible for the Native people to return to their tribes. Children born in the mission grew up learning from both the friars and their parents, but in time, the Native way of life was nearly forgotten. The friars thought they were helping the Ohlone by keeping them from their culture and lifestyle. Some Ohlone did not like this rule, or any of the rules that were imposed on them at the mission. In secret, they practiced their own beliefs and planned to escape.

At the mission, friars taught neophytes how to be more like the Spanish in how they spoke, what they ate, how they dressed, and their religious beliefs and practices.

5
Early Days of the Mission

BUILDING BEGINS

By the end of July 1797, several temporary structures had been built. This included living quarters for the friars and the neophytes, a guardhouse, a storehouse, a building in which the soldiers lived, and a fenced-in area for livestock. Before long, construction on the permanent buildings began. It was then decided by the missionaries that the mission would be built in the shape of a rectangle rather than the traditional **quadrangle**. The first structure standing was the church: a simple building with only three windows. The ceiling was 24 feet (7.3 m) high and the walls were 4 feet (1.2 m) thick. The church boasted a bell tower that rose above the height of the building's roof. The missionaries later decided to lower the tower to match the height of the church loft, as it stood at many other missions. San José's permanent church was completed in 1809. By 1810, sixty *rancherías*, or ranches for the neophytes, had been built. As the mission's population grew over the next fifteen years, new rancherías were added.

The entire mission site was completed in 1827. Among the buildings constructed were a guardhouse, a guesthouse, and a

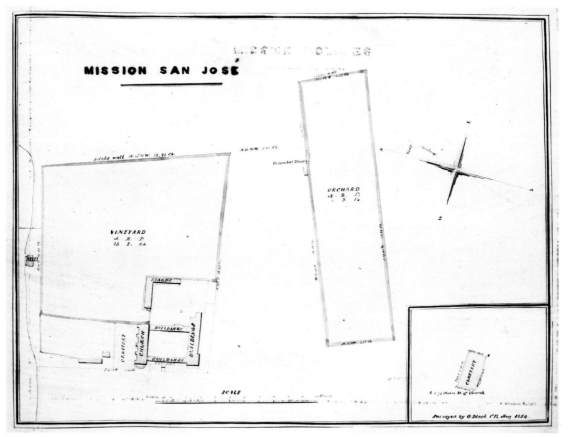

This layout of the mission grounds was drawn in 1854 and detailed how the mission looked at that time.

monjerío (meaning a women's dormitory). A soap factory and tannery were also included in the design. An aqueduct, or water system, stood behind the mission. In the front of the mission was a fountain, complete with a *lavandería*, or a huge basin used for washing clothes and bathing.

CROPS AND ANIMALS

Many crops were grown and animals were raised throughout Mission San José's years of existence. The main crops produced were barley, corn, beans, and other vegetables—often in far greater amounts than any other mission. Other important resources were tree orchards. Because the mission was founded on hilly land with rich soil for planting, olive trees and fruit trees, as well as a vineyard, were grown and cared for at the mission. This meant the missionaries and neophytes could produce large amounts of olive-based and fruit-based foods, as well as their own wine.

Animals were also important to the mission. Over the years the missionaries and neophytes raised many herds of cattle, sheep, and horses. Records show the amount of livestock held by Mission San José was in the upper 25 percent of all missions.

OTHER TRIBES AT SAN JOSÉ

The Ohlone was not the only Native tribe to live at Mission San José. Although they made up a large majority of the neophyte population (because they lived so close to the mission), over time other Native groups from the Miwok, Patwin, and Northern Valley Yokut tribes were also brought to the mission.

LEADING THE MISSION

Fray Barcenilla and Fray Merino led the mission from 1797 to 1806. They were both eager to preach, but each had skills that worked differently to help the Native people. Fray Barcenilla took on the spiritual matters at the mission, such as saying Mass and preaching, while Fray Merino helped develop the crops. It was hard work, however.

In 1806, Fray Barcenilla left the mission. Two new friars, Fray Buenaventura Fortuni and Fray Narciso Durán, then took over.

Both men were energetic, talented, and knowledgeable. Together they worked at Mission San José for 27 years and experienced some of the mission's best and worst times. They trained the Native people at the mission in many trades, from weaving and blacksmith work to furniture building and shoemaking. The women were taught to wash clothes, sew, and cook. Fray Durán also taught the Native people about Spanish music. He was known among the missions as a naturally gifted musician and passed his enthusiasm on to the Native people. Fray Durán assembled a church choir and an orchestra, which rehearsed in the inner court of the rectangle. He taught the neophytes to read music, sing in harmony, and play instruments. At first the neophytes creatively built their own musical instruments—as they had done in their own villages. But New Spain later supplied the mission with violins, flutes, and other instruments.

THE FIRST YEARS UNDER NEW LEADERSHIP

The first few years of frays Fortuni and Durán's leadership were not easy. In 1806, an epidemic of smallpox and measles struck the neophytes of the mission. As many of the neophytes had not developed immunity to diseases brought over by the Spanish missionaries, more than 150 Native people living at San José died. This loss of life was devastating not only to the neophytes who survived but also to the missionaries who had struggled to convert them. The epidemic spread beyond the Natives at the mission, affecting the tribes of Ohlone living nearby.

6
Daily Life at Mission San José

DAILY LIFE FOR THE NATIVE PEOPLE

Daily life at Mission San José, as well as at the other Alta California missions, varied little, except on holidays. This was a big adjustment for the Native people who lived there, since they were used to following their own rules and traditions in their own villages.

© PENTACLE PRESS

Once neophytes were baptized, they came to the missions where the friars made them keep strict schedules of prayer and work.

The daily schedule was highly structured and activities often revolved around the ringing of the bells. Every mission had at least two bells. They were important to all who lived and worked there, as each signaled important parts of the day: the first acknowledged time to pray, and the next—work, mealtimes, and rest.

A typical day began shortly after sunrise, when all the mission occupants went to the mission church to pray. An hour later, the bell rang for breakfast. Usually the meal was a large bowl of *atole*, a porridge made from corn. By 7 a.m., the workday began.

Male neophytes and soldiers typically worked in the fields or at building structures around the mission. Women usually participated in domestic chores, such as cooking and weaving. Before the indigenous women arrived at Mission San José, they and their ancestors had woven baskets from plants and had made cloth from fur and feathers. The Spanish, however, introduced them to weaving looms, spinning wheels, and materials such as cotton and wool, from which they learned to weave blankets and clothing. Children helped where they could, and often spent large parts of the day learning Spanish and studying the Catholic teachings.

The first break was at noon, when everyone ate lunch—usually a corn-based meal with a portion of beef and vegetables. Then they took a *siesta*, or nap. Everyone returned to work around 2 p.m. Three hours later the missionaries held prayers and devotions, and lessons and readings from the Bible. At 6 p.m. the dinner bell rang, and the rest of the evening was free time, which included dancing, games, or relaxation. The bell signaling bedtime rang at 8 p.m. for the women and at 9 p.m. for the men.

DAILY LIFE FOR THE FRIARS

Friars usually spent their days between prayer and running the mission. They attended to crops, buildings, and other areas such as finance and ensuring that the livestock were well. But the most important responsibility held by the friars was to educate the neophytes in their new religion. They taught them prayers and songs to worship God. The missionaries also led the young children in religious studies each morning and afternoon while the adults worked.

While the missionaries never benefitted financially from the Native people's work, they had to make sure the neophytes learned a trade so the mission could make money. The more neophytes able to create items, the more business for the mission. Because money was important to maintain the mission, it was important that the neophytes continue to work and live there. Many neophytes, however, missed the families they had left behind and the lifestyle they had led, so they tried to escape. The friars were responsible for disciplining those neophytes who did not perform their jobs or who tried to escape to their villages. The missionaries had the soldiers help in this area, tasking them to locate the neophytes who ran away. They would often punish the runaways as well. Sometimes other neophytes would join the search for those who had escaped.

Neophytes who worked hard to please the missionaries were free from harm, but those who longed for their old way of life had to deal with beatings or even being jailed and locked in shackles.

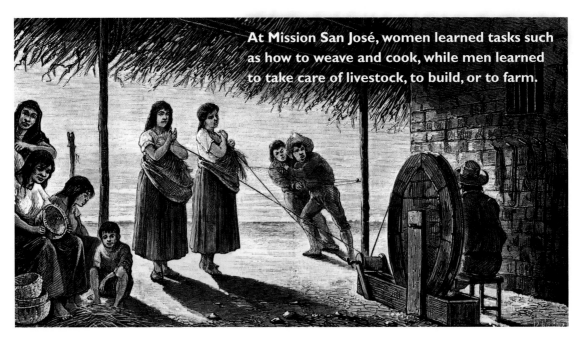
At Mission San José, women learned tasks such as how to weave and cook, while men learned to take care of livestock, to build, or to farm.

MORE WORK FOR THE NEOPHYTES

Neophytes labored at a number of tasks to keep the mission running. They learned to weave, farm, grow and cultivate gardens, tan leather, and make tools. Raising cattle was also important to the survival of all the missions. Cattle meat was used for food while hides were used to cover the frames of beds and the seats of chairs. Some hides were turned into buckets or nailed to doorframes to make doors. Hides were valuable and the missions traded them for other things that they needed.

As the years passed, the growth of the mission population slowed due to disease and the overall living conditions at the mission. Many neophytes were tasked to recruit others into the mission system. They were sent out to their old villages and to other tribes miles away with orders to return with new neophytes. Often, recruits were brought back against their will.

7
Troubles and Hardships

TOUGH TIMES

The missions of Alta California provided each Native American who joined with food, shelter, formal education, and protection from settlers and traders who did not always treat the Natives with respect or kindness. However, this lifestyle was very different from the one the Native Americans were used to. When the missionaries first arrived, the tribes could not foresee that they would lose their freedom, be forced to abandon their way of life, and be held inside the missions against their will.

Although many neophytes attempted to run away, others stayed willingly at the missions. Some enjoyed positive relationships with the friars, who wanted to protect and teach the Native people, not harm them. Despite their intentions, the friars did not understand that the neophytes deserved to live the way they always had and that their culture was just as valuable as the Spanish culture. This led to uncomfortable, and sometimes terrible, situations. Each time someone escaped there would be a punishment. Over time, many of the Native people living at San José became unhappy, stopped believing in what was being taught, and wanted to leave.

DISEASE AND POPULATION LOSS

The biggest problem at Mission San José, and at every other Alta California mission, was the threat of disease for the indigenous Californians. When the Spanish came over from Europe, they brought with them illnesses such as measles, smallpox, pneumonia, and mumps. The Native people had never been exposed to these diseases. Their immune systems were not equipped to fight them and thousands died. In fact, because of these diseases, the Native Californian population was drastically reduced throughout this time in history.

In 1805, Spanish soldiers unknowingly brought measles and smallpox to Mission San José. By 1810, the San José mission population had dropped from 800 to 545. Hundreds of California tribes had been affected by the sudden rise in disease. Many of the Native people, fearing the illnesses would take their lives, had fled.

THE UPRISING AT SAN JOSÉ

This unhappiness and hardship may have sparked the most famous mission uprising, which took place at Mission San José between 1828 and 1829. Estanislao, a respected and popular neophyte who had grown up under the mission system, led the **revolt**.

Born among the Yokuts in California's San Joaquin Valley in about 1800, Estanislao had lived at the mission from a young age. He was well liked by his peers and the friars, and had been elevated to the role of *alcalde*—meaning the administrative and judicial head of a town or village in Spain or in areas under Spanish control or influence. This was the highest rank a neophyte could have at the mission. Estanislao demonstrated great leadership skills and was awarded limited authority over the other neophytes.

While the exact reason that spurred Estanislao's actions are unknown, key facts are clear. In 1828, Fray Durán, who was running the mission at the time, gave Estanislao permission to visit his people, who lived inland from the coast, in the San Joaquin Valley. Instead of returning to the mission after the visit, Estanislao sent word to San José that he would not be coming back. He had tired of mission life and the structure that was forced upon him. He gathered forces of non-mission Natives, some neophytes from the

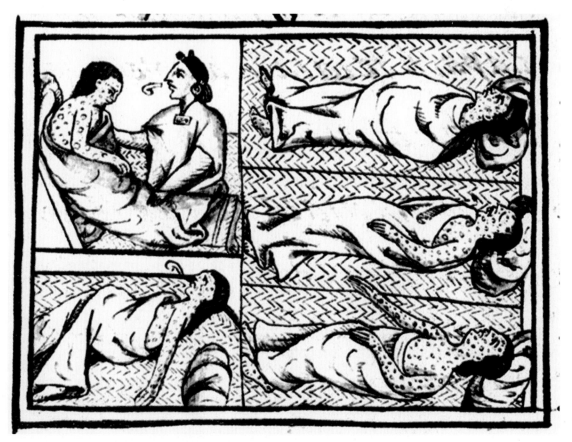

Diseases such as smallpox affected and killed many Native people.

Estanislao was leader of an uprising at San José.

San José mission and some from other northern California missions, and camped east of San Francisco Bay. They planned to attack and seize the mission, wanting to give it back to the Native people. For several months the group prepared for battle. During this time, soldiers around San José challenged the settlers in the area to find and capture Estanislao. They tried twice and failed on both occasions. Finally, in May of 1829, the Mexican government sent a young lieutenant named Mariano Vallejo and nearly all other northern California troops to capture Estanislao and his men.

A battle between the two groups left many of Estanislao's warriors dead. Estanislao himself, however, had escaped and returned to the San José mission, seeking forgiveness. Many soldiers and others wanted him killed for his actions. Instead, Fray Durán convinced the governor to pardon Estanislao, who remained at the mission until his death from smallpox in 1832.

This revolt proved the worst since the 1824 uprising at missions Santa Inés, La Purísima, and Santa Bárbara. During these events, a large neophyte population from the Chumash tribe seized control of the missions and burned many of the buildings before being persuaded to return to the missions once again as neophytes. These events proved that the Native people were becoming more and more unhappy with the mission system. Before long, something had to be done to restore peace.

8
Secularization

CHANGING TIMES

As the 1820s dawned, Mission San José had one of the strongest economies of all the missions. It was self-sufficient, producing enough goods to trade with the outside world, and growing the food necessary to feed everyone who lived there.

In 1821, Spain lost the Mexican War of Independence, and Alta California became part of Mexico. This had a destructive effect on the California mission system.

Mexico became its own country in 1821 and took over the mission lands.

In 1833, the Mexican government passed a law called the Act of Secularization. Secularization meant taking financial control of the missions away from the Catholic Church. Many Franciscan friars were removed from the missions and sent back to Spain. Replacing them were Mexican priests who had different ways of managing the missions. This also meant that the missions would no longer be used to convert indigenous Californians to Christianity, and the neophytes living there would be free to leave.

The neophytes had mixed feelings about their newfound freedom. Some were eager to leave the structured setting, while others were at a loss for what their future would hold without the support of the missions. Secularization forced them to make a change.

Some converted Native Americans returned to their villages or went to work at ranches, where they were often mistreated and underpaid. Others remained at the secularized mission because they had nowhere else to go. Many of their villages no longer existed, and the skills, languages, and traditions of their ancestors were mostly forgotten. Without their own culture, many indigenous Californians did not have the means to live better lives in freedom than they did at the missions.

Mexico's original intention of secularization was to turn the mission lands over to the Native people, but this did not happen. In April 1832, José Figueroa was appointed governor of the California territory. Soon after, Figueroa began to secularize the

After secularization, many neophytes left the mission, looking for new places to live and new jobs in the ranches and towns nearby.

Mission San José suffered significant damage from the Hayward earthquake in 1868.

missions. He had never planned to turn the rich lands over to the Native Californians, who had made it their home for centuries. Instead Figueroa sold the lands for a huge profit, often taking the cattle and other mission assets for himself.

SECULARIZATION OF MISSION SAN JOSÉ

Mission San José was secularized in 1834. Soon after, many neophytes left. In the years that followed, the mission's buildings were vandalized and the bricks and tiles taken to make settlers' homes. In 1848, the mission became a general store and hotel for gold seekers. Then, in 1853, three years after California became the thirty-first state, the mission became a town church called Saint Joseph's. It remained until 1868, when the Hayward earthquake caused great damage to its buildings.

MISSION SAN JOSE
43300

Today Mission San José has been restored, and it remains as a place to tour and learn about California's past.

9
The Mission Today

A VISIT TO MODERN MISSION SAN JOSÉ

Today's visitors to Mission San José can admire the building's white adobe walls and deep-red tile roof. The mission, in the early 1980s, underwent complete reconstruction. This included the building of an authentic mission church on the foundation of the original **adobe** church.

REBUILDING THE MISSION

The church's first permanent structure, completed in 1809, was destroyed during the 1868 Hayward earthquake. The earthquake affected many people and buildings throughout the San José area. However, unlike some of the buildings in the region, the church was soon replaced. A wooden Gothic-style church was constructed on top of the old church's foundation. However, it was not the same, and much of the church's original charm was lost with the new design.

Plans to duplicate the original Ohlone-built church began in 1973. In 1982, the wooden church was moved to another site, so that the reconstruction of the authentic-looking adobe mission church could begin. Three years later, the reconstructed Mission San José was complete. The groups supporting the restoration—the Committee for the Restoration of Mission San José and the Diocese of Oakland—saw to it that tools similar to those used by the missionaries and the Ohlone were used in the rebuilding process.

THE PRESENT-DAY MISSION

Today the rooms in which the missionaries once slept are a part of a small museum. The church continues to hold services in its **sanctuary**, and is an active member of St. Joseph's Parish. The mission also offers tours year-round to many students and tourists who want to learn more about the mission's past.

The four bells that hung in the original adobe church were dispersed to other churches after the earthquake. During the reconstruction of Mission San José, the same four bells were returned to the mission and hung in the newly restored tower.

Like the other twenty missions built along the California coast, Mission San José played a vital role in the development of California. The Spanish introduced farming and wine production methods, which are important to the state's economy today. The Spanish also encouraged new cities and towns to be built throughout California.

Visitors or those new to California may notice that several streets, cities, parks, and schools are named for important Spanish or Native American influences. These places serve as a reminder of the Spanish and Native people who helped make California what it is today.

10
Make Your Own Mission Model

To make your own model of the San José mission, you will need:

- Foam Core board
- scissors
- cardboard
- glue
- tape

- Popsicle sticks
- white and brown paint
- sand
- miniature trees and flowers

DIRECTIONS

Adult supervision is suggested.

Step 1: Cut a piece of Foam Core to 21" × 10" (53.3 × 25.4 centimeters) to use as a base.

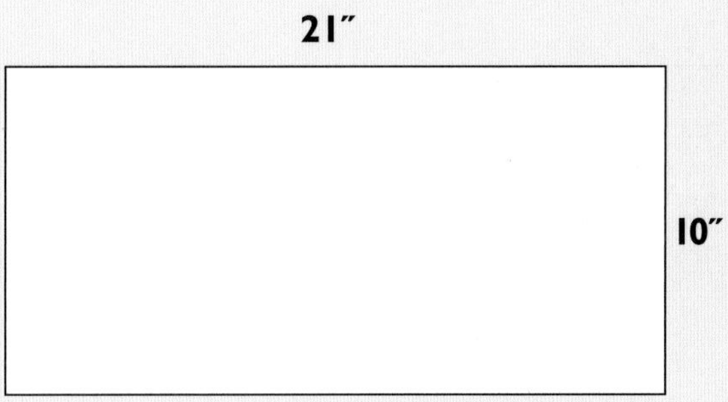

21″

10″

Step 2: To make the sidewalls of the church, cut four pieces of cardboard to measure 6" × 8" (15.2 × 20.3 cm).

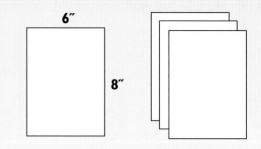

Step 3: Choose one of the cardboard pieces for the front wall of the church. Cut a door and a window into the front wall.

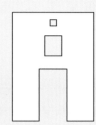

Step 4: Using glue, attach the front, back, and side walls of the church together. Tape the inside corners. Attach the church building to the Foam Core base.

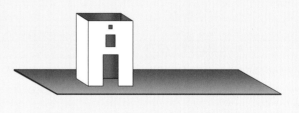

Step 5: Cut two cardboard triangles for the support walls to be added to the side of the church. One should measure 6" (15.2 cm) in height. The other should measure 4" (10.2 cm) in height.

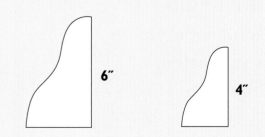

Step 6: Glue the support walls so that they stick out from one of the side walls of the church.

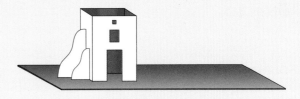

Step 7: Cut a piece of cardboard for the church roof measuring 8.5" × 7.5" (21.5 × 19 cm). Fold in half lengthwise, so that the roof will be pointed. Cut another piece of cardboard, measuring 11.5" × 6" (29.2 × 15.2 cm), for the roof of the friars' quarters. Fold in half, lengthwise.

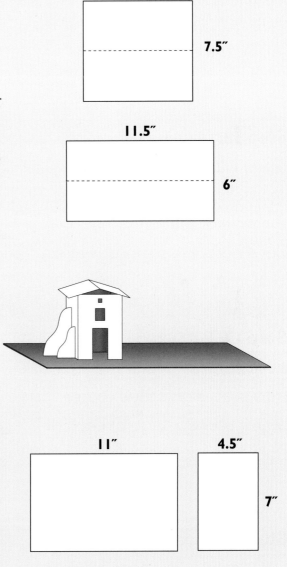

Step 8: Glue the roof to the church.

Step 9: For the missionary quarters, cut two long cardboard walls that measure 11" × 7" (27.9 × 17.8 cm). Cut a third piece for the end wall that measures 4.5" × 7" (11.4 × 17.8 cm).

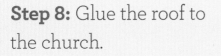

Step 10: Cut four small rectangular windows into one of the long walls.

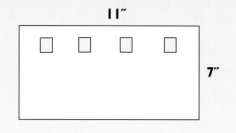

Step 11: Cut a door into the small end wall. Cut a window above the door.

Step 12: Glue together the three walls of the missionary quarters and attach them to the side of the church that does not have support walls.

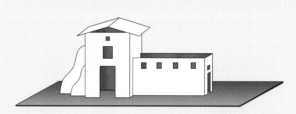

Step 13: Paint two Popsicle sticks brown. Break the sticks into pieces and glue them along the top edge of each of the windows and doors.

Step 14: Mix the sand with white paint. Paint the mission walls with this mixture.

Step 15: Glue the friar quarter's roof onto the building. Paint both roofs brown.

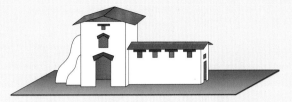

Step 16: Decorate the mission grounds with trees, rocks, and flowers.

Model of Mission San José when complete.

Key Dates in Mission History

1492	Christopher Columbus reaches the West Indies
1542	Cabrillo's expedition to California
1602	Sebastián Vizcaíno sails to California
1713	Fray Junípero Serra is born
1769	Founding of San Diego de Alcalá
1770	Founding of San Carlos Borroméo del Río Carmelo
1771	Founding of San Antonio de Padua and San Gabriel Arcángel
1772	Founding of San Luis Obispo de Tolosa
1775–76	Founding of San Juan Capistrano
1776	Founding of San Francisco de Asís
1776	Declaration of Independence is signed

1777	Founding of Santa Clara de Asís
1782	Founding of San Buenaventura
1784	Fray Serra dies
1786	Founding of Santa Bárbara
1787	Founding of La Purísima Concepción
1791	Founding of Santa Cruz and Nuestra Señora de la Soledad
1797	Founding of San José, San Juan Bautista, San Miguel Arcángel, and San Fernando Rey de España
1798	Founding of San Luis Rey de Francia
1804	Founding of Santa Inés
1817	Founding of San Rafael Arcángel
1823	Founding of San Francisco Solano
1833	Mexico passes Secularization Act
1848	Gold found in northern California
1850	California becomes the thirty-first state

Glossary

adobe (uh-DOH-bee)
Sun-dried bricks made of straw, mud, and sometimes manure.

Alta California (AL-tuh ka-luh-FOR-nyuh) The area where the Spanish settled missions, today known as the state of California.

claim (KLEYM) To assert that one rightfully owns something; to say that something belongs to you or that you deserve something.

convert (kon-VERT) To cause someone to change beliefs or religions.

friar (FRY-ur) A brother in a communal religious order. Friars can also be priests.

mission (MIH-shun) A religious community.

missionary (MIH-shuh-nayr-ee) A person who teaches his or her religion to people who have different beliefs.

neophyte (NEE-uh-fyt) A Native American who has converted to another religion.

quadrangle (KWAH-drayn-gul) The square at the center of a mission that is surrounded by four buildings.

revolt (ree-VOLT) To turn away from and fight against a leader.

sanctuary (SANK-choo-wehr-ee) A sacred place, such as a church.

secularize (SEH-kyoo-luh-rize) A process by which the mission lands were made to be nonreligious.

self-sufficient (SELF-suh-FIH-shent) Able to provide for one's own needs without outside aid.

shaman (SHAH-min) A medicine man or woman who is thought to use magic to heal the sick and control other events in people's lives.

tule (TOO-lee) Reeds used by Native Americans to make houses and boats.

Pronunciation Guide

convento (kon-BEN-toh)

El Camino Real (EL kah-MEE-noh RAY-al)

fiesta (fee-EHS-tah)

fray (FRAY)

lavandería (lah-ban-deh-REE-ah)

monjerío (mohn-hay-REE-oh)

pueblo de indios (PWAY-blo de IN-dee-ohs)

ranchería (rahn-cheh-REE-ah)

rancho (RAHN-choh)

Find Out More

To learn more about the California missions, check out these books, videos, and websites.

BOOKS

Beebe, Rose Marie and Robert M. Senkewicz (trans.). *Testimonios: Early California Through the Eyes of Women, 1815–1848*. Berkley, CA: Heydey Books, 2006.

Gendell, Megan. *The Spanish Missions of California*. New York, NY: Scholastic, 2010.

Gibson, Karen Bush. *Native American History for Kids*. Chicago, IL: Chicago Review Press, 2010.

Kalman, Bobbie. *Life of the California Coast Nations*. New York, NY: Crabtree Publications, 2004.

White, Tekla. *San Francisco Bay Area Missions*. Minneapolis, MN: Lerner Publishing, 2008.

VIDEOS

"Missions of California: Father Junípero Serra"
Produced by Chip Taylor Productions
This 11-minute, full-color video features photographs of Fray Serra, detailed maps, and beautiful scenery from many of the missions he founded. This video should be available at your local library.

WEBSITES

A Virtual Tour of California Missions

www.missiontour.org/sanjose/history.htm

Understand key events in the mission of San José by reading this detailed timeline of the mission's history.

California Mission Internet Trail

www.escusd.k12.ca.us/mission_trail/MissionTrail.html
Discover a map of the mission system and quick and easy facts for each mission.

California Missions Resource Center

www.missionscalifornia.com

Interact with a mission timeline, videos, and photo gallery and unlock key facts about each mission in the California mission system.

Mission San José

www.missionsanjose.org

Learn about the history of Mission San José and what it is like today.

National Park Service – Ohlone and Coast Miwoks

www.nps.gov/goga/historyculture/ohlones-and-coast-miwoks.htm

Read about the Ohlone people, what they believe in, and how they lived prior to the Spanish.

Index

Page numbers in **boldface** are illustrations.